GOD'S MIRACLE OF FAITHFULNESS

IN THE MATTER OF

THE JEWISH PEOPLE & ISRAEL

Dr. E. E. DeWitt

REL067030: Religion: Christian Theology – Apologetics.

ISBN: 979-8-9866583-2-2

All Scripture quotes are from the King James Bible except those verses compared and then the source is identified.

Address All Inquiries To:
THE OLD PATHS PUBLICATIONS, Inc.
142 Gold Flume Way
Cleveland, Georgia, U.S.A. 30528
Web: www.theoldpathspublications.com
E-mail: TOP@theoldpathspublications.com

Links to Distributors may be found on The Old Paths Publications website along with Sample pages, here:

http://theoldpathspublications.com/Pages/BookStore.htm

TABLE OF CONTENTS

INTRODUCTION

[This work was prepared for the 2022 Dean Burgon Society Bible Conference.]

GREETINGS

Greetings in the Name of the Lord Jesus Christ! Isn't it a great privilege that we are able to say that in truth! No question mark is placed after that last sentence as it was not a question; it is, rather, a statement of glorious truth!

You know, of course, why we end our prayers with the phrase "In the Name of Jesus." It isn't using His Name as a talisman; it is because by invoking His Name in such a manner we are making the claim that we believe we are speaking things that are in His Will and Purposes.

THROUGH A GLASS DARKLY

Do you understand why the world at large is unable to make that greeting in truth? They do not know Him in His Biblical fulness. They have no experiential knowledge of His will and His fulness. They do not know Him in the power, glory and position as Savior, not just of the World but also of their own eternal and un- redeemed soul.

The world speaks of translations made so that the unsaved will desire to read those words of God. Folks, the unsaved are not going to read the Words of Scripture as those Words, which are accurately the holy words of The (exclusive and ultimately glorious, God. He is not "a god" of just anything as He is The God of Reality and Creation.)...He is The God of True Scripture.

Sin separates the unregenerate from the ultimate pureness of God. That reality of sin separates the lost sinner from the Words of Life. They may well read even the True Words of Scripture. But they read those Words with the hope of pacifying a god of wrath rather than praising The God of Grace and Mercy.

We may well see *"through a glass darkly"* at times. But we can always see through a glass that is illuminated by the work of the Holy Spirit of The God Who loves us and dwells within us as adopted children of His. I think to Revelation 13:8 when I consider the Cross of Christ. "And all that dwell upon the earth, whose names are not written in the book of life of the Lamb slain from the foundation of the world."

Notice the scope of that one verse. It ranges from pre-creation of the earth where Jesus, looking down throughout the history of creation, saw the sin of man. The only remedy for this Satan inspired, but mankind implemented, situation involved the events of Calvary; creation continued with that reality fully understood.

Can we even begin to understand the ultimate love of God? That love was never based upon what we may have done. Indeed, what we did only served to make spiritual necessity of that which Jesus experienced at Calvary – the pain, the degradation, the humiliation of a brutal physical death before His mortal enemies. Calvary was the natural outgrowth of what we had really done. Can any of us really say "natural outgrowth" without considering the depth of His love and mercy?!

JACOB'S TROUBLE

That verse continues up until the time of the Great Tribulation, the Time - Jeremiah 30:7 - of Jacob's Trouble. Even at that late point in the history of this planet, there are still people who will scoff at Jesus and give their worship to the Beast and Antichrist. People who are gripped in sin will not follow the Savior! Nor will they be willing to accept the True Words of God without a miracle of grace wherein the Holy Spirit of God allows His Words to invade the domain of

Satan and allow the real Words of the Real Scripture to begin to melt those sin-encrusted hearts and allow the message of the gospel to lead them from dry *religion* into a saving *relationship* with the Master of our souls, the Lord Jesus Christ.

WHY THE POWERLESS CHURCH?

Why is the church, as an institution, seen as so powerless in this day? Part of this is, of course, that Satan continues his own nefarious work among the culture of the day. But Satan is powerless against the Power of God. We, even of so many of the fundamentalists, have departed from the Words of God and lusted after the words of man in the errant *translations* of the critical text. Our abandonment of the powerful Words of God has removed much of the power of our witness into the world. Our rejection of the true inspired and preserved Words of God, as evidence of our trust in HIM, and His power to preserve, has robbed us of the Words of Life.

More than just this, we have not utilized the Power of God by a holy reliance upon the Holy Spirit of God. Oh, the charismatic crowd has misrepresented the Spirit as they seem to make Him a veritable plaything of a magic act. Folks, the Holy Spirit of God is given to lead us into truth. (John 14:26)

He is not to be used as a talisman to call in as a *first responder* to make our life easier. That He will do as we trust Him and His influence. His influence is to remind us of the Words of God. (John 14:26) Our attempts at personal work and soul winning is often hampered by our refusal to pray for the souls of those we attempt to evangelize,

On the Cross Jesus shouted out, "My God, my God. Why hast Thou forsaken me." Why did He say that? Had The Father dissolved the insoluble bond of the trinity? NO! Of course not! That was the first verse of the 22nd Psalm. It is a first verse of one of the Messianic Psalms. While on the Cross, while going through the death pangs of His physical existence, Jesus was witnessing to the fact that He was the Messiah of God. He was, in effect, still calling men and women to Himself for their salvation from sin.

By the way, we must ask ourselves why Jesus, in the agony of His physical death did not quote that verse from the Greek? Are we not reminded that the Jews had so abandoned the Hebrew, that the Septuagint had replaced the Hebrew of the original autographs of Scripture. However, it was those originally inspired Words which bore the mark of the Inspiration of God.

We are often told that even Jesus and His closest followers had abandoned the "old" bible of the day for a new translation. And, yet, here at the end of His physical life, Jesus reverted back from the "new translation" to the "old fashioned Bible" with its inspired Words intact. Maybe we need to rethink a lot we've been fed about the Septuagint.

It is a great joy to be at a meeting such as this where the children of God have gathered together to pray and sing His praises as we hear the truth of the works of God in joyous obedience to the Lord and the Words He has inspired and blessed. We gather to give worshipful study of those wonderful Words of Life.

With no apologies to Walt Disney and the company which bears his name, this is the happiest place on earth. What great glory we are allowed to share as servants of the Most High God. Once again, no question mark either used or needed to that quiet and joyful consideration.

WE ARE A BLESSED PEOPLE!

Now to mention just a few of the people who have blessed us by their work in this Dean Burgon Society. These will not be mentioned in any special order. But, I feel, considering where this year's meeting is being held, I have need to mention Pastor Christian Spencer. I think it obvious that the attendees of this church understand how fortunate they are to be sitting under his ministry. Just to hear him speak is to understand how many hours he has spent in the study before he begins to stand in the pulpit. He is a master of his craft for the Master. It is obviously a labor of love to the work of the God of Love, and the Son Who died on that cruel Cross to offer us freely, salvation from our sins.

Sir, my military background showing respect to one who is my superior, you are one of my favorites.

I can't go on without mentioning Pastor Dan Waite. How he is missed by his absence today. We know that he misses the organization which he has so faithfully served these past years. Without his tireless efforts we would be a much smaller organization. He has done as much as anyone to make us what we are, today. I understand that the Lord is the real power which blesses us as a group. Dan has always been ready to work to the best of his ability for the good of the group and the love of the Lord Who loved him, first.

I cannot forget Dr. D. A. Waite. Without the efforts of him and his dear wife, we would, humanly speaking, have no DBS where to attend meetings. His energy and spiritual counsel have guided us from our inception as a group. He has been more than our leader, he has become a spiritual father, in a sense, to most of us.

I have recently been watching old reruns of "What's My Line," the old television quiz show from the 1950's and '60's. At one point Bennet Cerf introduced John Daly with this: "I wish to introduce our panel moderator with a quotation from Scripture. 'He uttereth a multitude of words, but he understandeth them not.'"

By the way, I tried to find that verse and it seems not to exist. However, with the multiplication of tomes self-identified as Scripture anything, anywhere may be possible.

Dr. Waite would never mistake *Poor Richard's Almanac* as Scripture. He knows what true Scripture says. He never uses a multitude of words. He well could, but he understands the imparting of knowledge must be ferried by clear communication. Had he ever used a "multitude of words," they would have all been presented in a way that his audience could have learned from the oration. Dr. Waite has been an articulate and trustworthy teacher to us for many years.

Dr. Waite, we will be true to the Lord as we attempt to continue your vision into this created world. Your vision of a pure Word is the vision of the Lord of that Word.

There are many more who could, and should, be mentioned. Space, and my tired typing fingers fail at this point. But each of you is important in this Work for the Lord. And that is what this is; it is a work FOR the Lord Who died for us. On purpose. He died in time so that we could live in eternity.

I WAITED FOR YOU

With all the above said, where is I? I know that is an improper sentence. Well, I is feeling improper as I miss being among you. I can only explain my absence by reminding you that I am a little stupid.   Not as stupid as my wife. She said "Yes," and then went through with the marriage ceremony.

We were married back in 1968 just twelve days before I boarded the plane to go to the war in Viet Nam. One year later I was to board another airplane to bring me back to her. I missed the plane.

I don't know how many of you have been in the military. They have a regulation somewhere that places great importance on a soldier being where he is told to be when he is told to be there. They talked with me for a few minutes!

Somewhere during my eventual flight home, I realized that by missing that first airplane, Linda would have no idea when I would return. I could surprise her and complain that she didn't even come out to the airport to welcome me back.

I got off the plane, with a dime in my pocket for the phone. It was a long time ago. I went into the air terminal to call a cab. There was Linda setting in the welcoming section waiting for me. "How did you know I was coming back tonight?"

Linda's reply, any of you preachers who want to relate this as an illustration have my permission. "I didn't know you were coming back tonight. I knew it would be sometime soon, so I just came out every night and waited for you."

I married very well; Linda didn't get near as good as I got!

DAISY, THE CAT, AND RACOONS

To further preface my excuse for not being here, I will explain that I mow the lawn in the pen where our dog, Daisy, spends her days. I pay a neighborhood kid to mow the rest of the yard; but I only trust me to mow inside that Dog pen.

Daisy is a very friendly dog. She loves people. If she approaches a stranger, unless they appear to harm one of "her" people, she will – at the most – try to get her front paws on their shoulders so she can lick their face. That is the total of her aggression. Still, she does hate lawn mowing machines. I think they hurt her ears. So, she tries to bite the lawn mower wheels. I am afraid that someone else, knowing her friendly nature and not her hatred of lawn mowing machines, will slice her jaw. I mow inside Daisy's pen.

There is one other thing that Daisy hates. Birds. We once raised chickens. They got lose inside Daisy's pen and we didn't need to feed her for a few days. Of course, after those few days we didn't collect as many eggs, either.

Daisy is not big on playing those "doggy games." For instance, don't even try to play "fetch" with her. If you throw a stick, Daisy will go get it. Don't bother waiting for her to bring it back. She won't. She figures that if you wanted it, you would have kept it.

Our cat is another problem. She has learned to open the back door so she can go outside. Since she can get out, she has never learned to shut the door. Cats are not good at learning many tricks. One seems to be the limit.

The upshot of this was, I got up early one morning and found the back door open and a couple of racoons in the room.

Back to my excuse, I was busy mowing with Daisy attacking that invading lawn mower machine. I kept telling her, "NO!," and attempting to finish the job. Finally, being frustrated with her inability to quiet the loud mower, Daisy decided to lick my face. She was just trying to get my attention.

The upshot of this was that I fell through the fence and into a ditch. Now, I am subject – at my age – to falling down. It's the getting back up part that I don't do well. Ethan, my son, had given me a thing that ties around my neck and holds my phone so I can call him to come and get me up.

I wasn't wearing it. Daisy, seeing my distress, had left to find help. At least, that's what I'm going to say. A passing motorist seemed to understand that I wasn't laying by the road to rest. The man sent his wife up to the front door to alert Ethan to my problem. Within 15 minutes of falling, Ethan had me back on my feet and Daisy in her indoor kennel.

Ethan told me to stop mowing for the night. We were going to the hospital ER. I am under a medication. It isn't a blood thinner; it is a clotting inhibiter. I am under strict orders from the VA doctors to go and be checked out at an ER if I fall down; well, at my age, when I fall down and am bruised. They are worried about internal bleeding. They took several hours to look me over and prescribe some sort of narcotic medicine that makes me run at 33 1/3 while the rest of the world is on a 78.

I am very hesitant to take their medicine. However, when I don't take it, the pain is very interesting. I wasn't at all sure that I wanted to make the bus trip all the way here.

EXCUSES. EXCUSES. EXCUSES.

Compounding this, I didn't really have a good message prepared. Or, a bad message, for that matter. I call that the Scarlette O'hara (I can't spell it but I can say it.) rational from "Gone with the wind." I can always worry about that tomorrow,

I have been working on a verse-by-verse commentary on the minor prophets. I did have some relevant material from the prophet Micah. Considering the amount of time, it takes me to type at this stage of life, I will submit the commentary from Micah 7:12-13 relating to the prophecy concerning,

"God's Miracle of Faithfulness in the Matter of the Jewish People and Israel."

GOD'S MIRACLE OF FAITHFULNESS

The prophecies of God, and His Book, are even more certain than the events related in tomorrow's newspaper: The fact that God has kept His promises to Israel stands as testimony that He will also keep His promises to us.

"Micah 7.12 "In that day also he shall come even to thee from Assyria, and from the fortified cities, and from the fortress even to the river, and from sea to sea, and from mountain to mountain."

[The pious Jew of antiquity only saw two epochs of human history. These were the pre-messianic and the Messianic ages. Which age is spoken of in this passage is up for debate. However, when we consider the time of the diaspora and view the places from which these people had repatriated themselves from the diverse destinations of that displacement of the people and to where they had returned, it is fairly easy to see this as the Kingdom Age wherein the restored Davidic King, Messiah, reigns is shown.

This is an event which will happen when Messiah, Jesus, has returned to the earth after that great Time of Tribulation. He will restore all Israel to the entire land which God has promised to His Covenant People. No longer will the people of this covenant wander over the earth. (By the way, I, personally see the Diaspora as part of the judgment for their forsaking the pure Words and worship of the Lord.) They will inhabit the entire Land of Promise under the restored Kingdom of David. The slice of land which they now occupy is only a small sliver of the land promised at the Word and promise of God. The Word of God will always ring true even as His promise is guaranteed by His own holiness and immutability.]

Micah 7.13 "Notwithstanding the land shall be desolate because of them that dwell therein, for the fruit of their doings." Cf **Isaiah 3:10-11; 56:9; Jeremiah 21:14; Micah 4:10; 5:13; 7:13**

ALIYAH, THE JEWISH RETURN

Is the present return of the Jew to his homeland a prelude to the second coming of Jesus to earth, to set up His Millennial Kingdom?

I believe that it is. One of the reasons lies in this very verse. The previous verse had spoken of that Kingdom Age. The present verse speaks of the devastated land that will greet the Jew as he returns to his ancestral land.

THE SHRINKING

It is rather easy to see the holocaust of Hitler's Germany as one of the greatest human tragedies recorded in the annals of history. It was so horrible that it gave the impetus which provided a picture of the outworking of the situation where a world that has shown extreme antisemitic bias for over two millennia of human history. But soon even that focus began to fade. The 45,560 square miles, nearly the size of the State of Pennsylvania in the United States, shrank to 23% of that mandate to only 10,478 square miles, of which 4,500 square miles was desert. (Gathered from *"It Is No Dream,"* McQuaid, Elwood, 2019. Available from The Friends of Israel Gospel Ministries, Bellmawr, New Jersey, USA) – As an aside, I heartily recommend this book which I freely admit provided much of the information used in my commentary on this verse!)

This *shrinking* may have been a blessing. The smaller size lends itself to a designation as a *"Jewish homeland"* and *"a Jewish state."* Indeed, the secular Jewish state of Israel sits, even today, within the confines of the Land which God has promised to the descendants of Abraham, Isaac and Jacob. It does not contain *all* of the Land of the promise of God. But all of the land occupied is part of the birthright of Israel.

Interestingly enough, after the first Zionist congress (August 29-31, 1897 in Basel, Switzerland, as organized by Theodore Hetzl), there was a renewed emphasis on buying land in the area of ancient Israel. Although the land may have seen the legal empowerment of the League of Nations implementing the spirit of the Balfour recommendations, the actual land so ceded was often the land already owned, via purchase, by the Jew. The land was happily sold at premium price but was, nonetheless, desert and swampland.

Therefore, that land to which the Jew returned was as described in verse 13. In *The innocents abroad*, the humorist Mark Twain reported his view of the land after a trip to the area in 1869, "It was a hopeless, dreary, heartbroken land… Over it broods the spell of a curse that has withered its fields and fettered its energies… (It is a land that sleeps) in the hush of a solitude that is inhabited only by birds of prey and skulking foxes." In short, the original Jewish settlers found a *holy land* of desert and swamp.

THE RESTORATION

As the hands, hearts and intellect of the Jew worked a miracle of restoration upon the land that had suffered ages of neglect and destruction at the hands of its previous occupants.

Consider a very surface look at the Revelation. There are those who would deny that the Jew is mentioned in that Book. Sort of a silly position to take considering that this is the Revelation of Jesus to John. Jesus, we may recall, was born into humanity as a Jew. (Galatians 4:4 and 5)

In the second and third chapter of Revelation, we find the Book addressed to seven churches which were planted by Jewish missionaries.

In the seventh chapter of the Book we find the 144,000 sealed witnesses all identified by the Jewish tribe of which they were members.

There is one more place where the Jewish nation is mentioned. Revelation 12:1 gives a sign. You can read the rest of this narrative down through verse ten, and following. The question arises as to who is the woman of whom this sign speaks

The Roman/ church would argue that this woman is the virgin Mary. This cannot be. This is called a "sign;" it is not any human person.

Many would argue that this concerns the church. Since the woman gives birth to Messiah, this cannot be. The church did not birth Christ; Christ gave birth to the Church. This sign is of the Jewish nation. Notice, as we continue to read in this twelfth chapter of Revelation that this woman (Israel) is protected even though she is under heavy persecution from Satan.

God promised, Genesis 12:1-3, that Abraham and his descendants would be blessed. Although terribly persecuted by Satan, the Jewish people are kept from extinction by the Spirit and Power of God. That is the only reason that we are able to see the evidence of their blessings in this day. We never find most of the other groups mentioned in the histories of the Old Testament mentioned as people groups in this day. The fact of the endurance of the Jewish people is testimony that they are still blessed of God. This is as God said it would be.

THE BALFOUR RESOLUTION

It might be good at this time to consider a short synopsis of the Balfour resolution which was presented near the conclusion of the First World War, at a time when the

Turkish califate was on the verge of collapsing.

"His Majesty's Government view(s) with favour the establishment in Palestine of a national home for the Jewish people, and will use their best endeavours to facilitate the achievement of this objective, it being clearly understood that nothing shall be done which may prejudice the civil and religious rights of existing non-Jewish communities in Palestine, or the rights and political status enjoyed by Jews in any other country."

It is worth noting that the State of Israel has always held to the spirit of the letter of this proclamation. For instance, the Jewish state is not responsible for the *refugee problem.*

However, in the ebb of time, it had become apparent that the British governments adherence to the spirit of Balfour had changed. The free emigration of the Jewish survivors from the holocaust of Germany was curtailed. One famous example concerned the ship, *Exodus,* with over four thousand survivors of the holocaust. The ship was rammed and denied permission to dock and disgorge its cargo of refugees. The ship's passengers were divided in three other vessels, and they were rerouted to France, from which they had originally set sail. My guess is that this was done because the ramming of the original ship had rendered it unseaworthy.

The overriding concern was that the emigration of Jewish people to Israel was being curtailed at this point in time, (1947), by the British Protectorate. The Jewish passengers did not want to return to France. They wanted to go home – to Israel. They refused to disembark from the ships. The French were loath to forcibly remove these Jewish holocaust survivors. Or, they didn't want them either. "So, the ships were directed to – of all places – Hamburg, Germany, where the authorities were less disposed to consider the passengers' desires." Imagine the horror of these Jewish people as they were deposited, against their will from the ships, into two internment camps inside Germany!

This incident should give some idea of just how many were making *Aliya to Israel* at this point. Indeed, after the Declaration of Statehood by Israel in 1948, the population of Israel had more than doubled at the end of 1951.

Much is often made of the Arab population which fled Israel soon after her independence as a reason for the lack of *refugee camps* in Israel as opposed to those same camps in the Arab lands. One must consider that the number of Jews coming to Israel from pogroms begun by the Arab nations toward the Jew in their land is roughly the same as the number of Arab citizens who fled Israel into the Arab lands at the time of her *War of Independence*.

The lack of refugee camps in Israel, as opposed to the number of refugee camps in the Arab nations is not due to a lack of humanity on the part of Israel as is the difference between the policy of assimilation toward the newcomers in Israel, and the lack of such policy among the Arab nations. Those tents set up for the refugees in Jordan, for instance, presents a propaganda picture for the world's press to paint a picture of the *heartless* Jews whether that be a true picture or not!

One of the things that greatly helps in this assimilation is that ancient Hebrew is the official language of Israel. Hebrew had not been an official language, except as used for religious purposes, (This in itself is interesting because we are often assured that the Septuagint was made necessary because the Jewish people needed a Greek translation in their synagogues because the Hebrew was no longer understood. Anything to sell some copies of the Critical Text.) since the failed revolt of Ben-Kobba in 135 A.D. This rebellion is, of current interest; this is especially so in its aftermath when the Romans renamed Galilee, "Palestine," after Israel's ancient enemy, the Philistines. Without this historical change, the Palestinians would be known as the Galileans.

ONLY HEBREW

In about 1881, Eliezer Ben-Yehuda (1858-1922) was one of the first to feel the raising steam of Zionism. He, and some of his friends, moved to Jerusalem and covenanted together to speak only Hebrew among themselves. There is a story that he once reprimanded his wife for singing a nursery song to his young child in German rather than in Hebrew.

Ben-Yehuda, his name means 'Son of Israel," was one of the first to realize the need for a common, uniting language for the coming State of Israel. Realize that this was nearly twenty years before the first Zionist Congress. His dictionaries combining the same early Hebrew of the prophets and *new* words added to the dictionary which needed to be added for the present age, are still used to this day. The ancient prophets, for instance, rarely spoke of airplanes and tanks.

The revival of the language, at the same historical time as the revival of the nation/state of Israel is a miracle that can only be explained by the God of History and His evident working within the world of humanity. Today Hebrew is the national language of Israel. It greatly aids the merging of so many people into one nation. Rather than building refugee camps, Israel builds one nation of people united by a common thread of culture, history and language. Many of the *kibbutzims* will offer a five-month intensive training in the language for the new-commers.

There is no need for refugee camps in Israel. They are one people, with one history, with one language, within one miracle land.

LEARN FROM THE JEW

There is much that we in this country could learn from the Jew.

Along with this I would only add one thing from a film produced by *The Friends of Israel* about the miraculous Six-Day War of 1967. When, Moshe Dayan first arrived at the Temple Mount, he was surprised to see the flag of Israel flying from the site. He immediately had it taken down. The *doctrine of stasis* was established which allowed the Muslim forces the right to maintain control over the Islamic *holy site*; this continues to this day.

Don't let anyone tell you that the Jew, this secular state of Israel, has no understanding or compassion for their Arab cousins of the world. We know, of course, that the day will come when Israel gains total control of the city of Jerusalem, to include the site of their rebuilt Temple.

Meanwhile, I would like to include one final verse from my commentary on Micah. Chapter one and verse fifteen reads:

"Micah 1.15 For the inhabitant of Maroth waited carefully for good: but evil came down from the LORD unto the gate of Jerusalem."

[There was no help to any of these cities sent from the capital of Jerusalem. There was no help because thousands of the Assyrian troops, apparently led by Rabshakah, had laid siege to Jerusalem. There were no troops that could be spared from Jerusalem. They were needed to defend capital, king and Temple. The people of Maroth, possibly the same as in Joshua 15:59, waited as patiently for the good news of a rescue party from Jerusalem, instead they recalled hearing the voice of the true prophet of God give forth the truth that God would judge the sins of the people. The people of Maroth probably did not hear that the king, Isaiah, and others were praying repentance and beseeching God for His hand of mercy. Although this did not come to them even on the wings of gossip, the evidence of God's mercy did show forth His power to save.

Now we look at Micah 5:2. Having two cities with the same name was not an unusual occurrence in an age of very slow travel, consider the prophecy of the birth of Jesus in Bethlehem. "But thou, Bethlehem Ephratah, though thou be little among the thousands of Judah, yet out of thee shall he come forth unto me that is to be ruler in Israel; whose goings forth have been from of old, from everlasting."

Consider also, Bethlehem of that the penman who gave us the location of the birth of Christ, gave us the exact location by adding that this Bethlehem was the one associated with Ephratah.]'

ABANDONMENT OF THE PURE WORDS

We can see some of the sin which caused the judgment of God to fall upon the Kingdom's of Israel and Judah. The base sin was that they had abandoned the pure Words of God and followed after a false religion of the culture of the lands around them.

Have we not done the very same thing as we have abandoned the pure words of God's Traditional Text, as given us in English by the translator's art in our Authorized, King James, Version? Instead, we have begun to worship from the tainted sanctuary of the Critical Texts' words of man. The entire rational for the Critical Text is that God either could not, or would not, preserve the Word's He labored to inspire. As such, we are left with an uninspired *bible*!

I'd like to reference just one more Bible verse.

Romans 11:25 – "For I would not, brethren, that ye should be ignorant of this mystery, lest ye should be wise in your own conceits; that blindness in part is happened to Israel, until the fulness of the Gentiles be come in."

THE CONCLUSION: MARANATHA

Folks, do you pray, "Maranatha?" Do you long for the return of the Savior to this world? Do you hopefully wait for the rapture of the church? Do You? If your answer is in the affirmative to these questions, there is one thing upon which you must major in your life. This can hasten the return of the Lord.

This isn't something I've made up. This is a guarantee of Scripture. What is that thing? It is simply the obeying the Word of the Lord to go out into the highways and compel them to come in. It is soul-winning!

Now, we do not know how many Gentiles have yet to be saved. We have no idea when that last soul to be saved will come in. We do know, the Scripture tells us that when the fulness of the Gentiles is "come in," that the Lord will open the eyes of the Jew unto their Messiah.

When this happens, Jesus, that very Messiah, will open the eyes of the Jew and work the great work of the New Covenant upon their hearts. At this point He will return to earth and establish His Millennial Reign.

We don't know when this will happen. Personally, I believe that this will be a Tribulation Era person who finds salvation in the Lord. Perhaps it will be from the efforts of those 144,000 Jews who will accomplish a feat in under seven years that we Gentiles have not accomplished in over 2,000 years. They will evangelize the world with the Good News that Jesus died in time so that others can live in eternity!

But, it will happen! We have God's guarantee of that!

Now, let us all say "Maranatha, Lord, come quickly!" Next, let's all go out and act as though we mean that! May we leave this meeting and go out into the world and be, simply, Christians. That means let us act with the fervor of Christ into the favor of Christ as we "Seek the sinners unto repentance!"

[As prepared for the 2022 Dean Burgon Society Bible Conference.]